This book belongs to

....

For Jack and his lion - K.P.

For Dalmas and Alex - our fantastic Kenyan Guides,
who taught me so much, and brought my love of Cats to life - B.H.

Published in 2024 by Welbeck Children's Books
An Imprint of Hachette Children's Books, Part of Hodder & Stoughton Limited
Carmelite House, 50 Victoria Embankment, London EC4Y 0DZ
www.welbeckpublishing.com
www.hachette.co.uk

Text © 2024 Kate Peridot
Illustration © 2024 Becca Hall

A CIP catalog record for this book is available from the British Library.

The website addresses (URLs) included in this book were valid at the time of going to press. However,
it is possible that the contents or addresses may have changed since the publication of this book.
No responsibility for any such changes can be accepted by either the author or the publisher.

ISBN 978 1 80453 571 4

Printed in China

1 3 5 7 9 10 8 6 4 2

Disclaimer: Any names, characters, trademarks, service marks and trade names detailed in this book
is the property of their respective owners and are used solely for identification and reference
purposes. This book is a publication of Welbeck Children's Books, part of Welbeck Publishing Group
and has not been licensed, approved, sponsored or endorsed by any person or entity.

Meet the CATS

KATE PERIDOT  BECCA HALL

W

WELBECK

Ahoy! Art Adventurers

Do you know your tiger stripes
from your leopard spots?

Join an adventure around the world
to draw the world's BIGGEST cats.

Our local guides promise it's going to be WILD
and there's a prize for the best cat drawing.

Sign up here.

This is the perfect vacation for you and your mom.

You both love drawing cats.

Reading books about cats.

Singing songs about cats.

Wearing clothes inspired by cats.

And your mom even drives a car named after a cat!

You're trying on your new hiking boots when your tickets arrive.
Eight amazing expeditions to find big cats in the wild!

What are you waiting for?
Drop Mr. Fluffles off at the cat sitter and get packing.

BIG CAT DRAWING SET

• art supplies

• camera and
zoom lens

• headlight

• binoculars

• water bottle

I can't wait to
draw my favorite cat.
I wish Mr. Fluffles was
coming too.

Welcome to the jungle. We climb into the tree house and get comfortable as night falls. The jungle comes alive with a chorus of *clicking, cheeping, hooting* animals. Suddenly, the hairs stand up on the back of our necks and we know we're being watched! We put on our night vision goggles. In the tree opposite, a black cat with gleaming eyes is staring at us.

Meet the BLACK PANTHER.

The black panther is a leopard with black fur.

He hunts at night. His black coat makes him almost invisible in the shadowy forest.

Powerful paws, sharp claws and a long tail are for climbing, balancing and hunting.

He prefers to pounce on his prey from above and drag his dinner into a tree so other animals can't steal it.

🐾 PREY:

antelope

rabbit

deer

monkey

fish

wild boar

🐾 DO PANTHERS ROAR?
Yes, but they can't purr.

🐾 RANGE:
Mountain savannas and forests of Central and West Africa, West and Southeast Asia, and India.

🐾 HOW TO DRAW PANTHER SPOTS:
From a distance, panthers look all black — but they are leopards, so have leopard markings of rosettes and spots in shades of black and dark brown.

Would you like to draw the black **panther**?

No, he's too sneaky.

Safe in the jeep we watch and wait a short distance from a water hole. As the hot sun begins to set, a large cat walks out of the long, dry grass. The wading birds flap away in alarm. She sniffs the air and looks at us for a moment, then she *chuff-chuffs*, and two cubs race to her side to drink at the water's edge.

Meet the TIGER.

The tiger is the largest big cat.

She prefers to hunt at dusk and dawn, and ambushes her prey from behind.

She loves to take baths to cool off and is a great swimmer.

Dad will sometimes share his dinner with his family, but he prefers to roam alone and must defend his territory from other males.

🐾 PREY:
Anything they can catch but wild boar and deer are their favorites.

wild boar

monkey

peacock

deer

fish

hare

🐾 HOW TO DRAW TIGER STRIPES:
Her orange coat patterned with long, dark stripes is a perfect disguise among the tall grass and forest underbrush. Rarely, tigers are born with black stripes against white fur.

🐾 DO TIGERS ROAR?
Yes, very loudly! Their roars can be heard almost 2 miles (mi) away. But they can't purr.

🐾 RANGE:
Forests, swamps and mountains of India, Bhutan, Nepal, Bangladesh, Southeast Asia and Russia.

Would you like to draw a **tiger**?

No, they are too big.

After a high-altitude climb, we camp out overnight in the Himalayan mountains. As dawn breaks, our guide wakes us up and we wiggle out of our tents, wrapped up warm because it's very cold. Below in the rocky valley, a herd of wild sheep graze. Our guide points to the cliff above them. Stepping gracefully from ledge to ledge is a ghostlike cat on the prowl.

Meet the SNOW LEOPARD.

His large eyes have great low-light vision.

A snow leopard is more closely related to a tiger than a leopard.

He has short forelegs and long hind legs to climb steep slopes. He can jump an incredible 30 feet (ft).

He travels great distances to find prey. When he catches a big meal, he stores it in a snow tunnel.

Wide, furry paws help him walk silently on the snow.

When he sleeps, he wraps his long, fluffy tail around his body to keep warm.

 **RANGE:**
Rocky valleys, ravines and cliffs
of the high mountains of India,
China and Russia.

 DO SNOW LEOPARDS ROAR?
No, but they have a very
loud YOWL and they do purr.

**HOW TO DRAW SNOW
LEOPARD SPOTS:**
His long, thick grayish-cream fur has dark rings
and spots to blend in with the snow and rock.

 **PREY:**

wild sheep

snow cock

ibex

marmot

hare

*Would you like
to draw the
snow leopard?*

*No, my
fingers are
too cold!*

deer

pika

With a *whoosh*, our hot-air balloon lifts off and we float over the savanna. Below, a cat with a golden mane leads his family out from the shade of a tree. He ROARS at the setting sun, letting the hyenas and other big cats know that this is his territory and he will defend it. When the lionesses have caught dinner, they step back and let him eat first.

Meet the LION.

Young males must leave the pride to find their own territory when they are two years old.

The pride mostly hunts from dusk until dawn, when it is cooler. During the day, they love to laze away together.

Lions live in family groups called prides which include up to five females and their cubs, and one or two adult male lions.

The lionesses work as a team to raise the cubs and to hunt large prey.

🐾 PREY:
Any meat will do, and a lion will steal a cheetah or leopard's dinner.

hare

zebra

wildebeest

warthog

antelope

giraffe

buffalo

🐾 RANGE:
The grassland savannas, scrub forests and desert edges of sub-Saharan Africa. The smaller Asian lion lives in the forests of western India.

🐾 DO LIONS ROAR?
Yes, loudly, but they can't purr.

🐾 HOW TO DRAW A LION'S MANE:
Male lions have distinctive golden manes that grow longer and darker with age. Rarely, lions are born white. Cubs have sandy-colored coats with spots which disappear as they grow.

*Do you want to draw a **lion**?*

***No**, he's too noisy!*

We're on safari and are stopping to watch the gazelles when a big cat leaps on the roof of our jeep. Don't worry, she's not interested in us. She's on the lookout for lunch. She jumps down, and with a sudden burst of speed chases after a fleeing gazelle. She must catch it because her hungry cubs are hiding in the grass nearby.

Meet the CHEETAH.

The cheetah is the fastest land mammal in the world. She can sprint from zero to 50 miles per hour (mph) in under three seconds and can reach top speeds of 75 miles.

She uses her tail like a rudder to change direction at high speeds.

Young adult cheetahs and males sometimes live and hunt in small groups called coalitions.

🐾 PREY:

gazelle

hare

bird

antelope

warthog

rabbit

🐾 DO CHEETAHS ROAR?

No, but they do purr.

Once a female has cubs, she lives and hunts alone.

🐾 HOW TO DRAW CHEETAH SPOTS:

She has black teardrop markings on her face and thousands of spots on her light tan coat. Cubs have a smoky-colored fluffy coat called a mantle which blends in with the desert scrub and long grasses.

🐾 RANGE:

The grassland savannas and scrub forests in parts of northwestern, eastern and southern Africa, and Iran.

Would you like to draw a cheetah?

No, she's too fast!

Pull on your snowsuit and click on your skis to glide along silvery moonlit trails. This cat's hard to track so our guide follows the hoofprints of its favorite food, reindeer. We hide behind a snowdrift and wait, watching the herd graze. Just as our fingers and toes go numb, a cat slinks out of the forest and creeps toward the herd. They catch his scent, surround their calves and lower their horns!

Meet the LYNX.

His tail is very short with a black tip.

With great night vision and hearing, he can detect the slightest movement.

His broad furry paws are like snowshoes and help him walk silently on top of the snow.

He likes to stalk and ambush his prey, but he won't waste energy chasing it.

He roams a large territory and lives alone, except when looking for a mate.

He sleeps in rock and tree crevices.

🐾 HOW TO DRAW LYNX SPOTS AND TUFTS:

His coat is golden brown in summer and changes to a thicker silver-brown in winter. It has mottled black spots. He has distinctive tufts of black fur on the tops of his ears and a ruff of fur around his face.

🐾 DO LYNX ROAR?

No, but they do purr.

🐾 RANGE:

Broadleaf forests with dense shrubs and tall grasses in Scandinavia, parts of southern and eastern Europe, central and east Asia, Canada and Alaska. (There are three species of lynx: the Canadian lynx, the Eurasian lynx and the smaller Iberian lynx).

🐾 PREY:

fish

reindeer

fox

mouse

red squirrel

chamois

bird

snow hare

red deer

Would you like to draw a lynx?

No, he's too shy.

A wildlife photographer invited us to hike with him to a secret hide in the Rocky Mountains. It overlooks a wild cat's den. As evening shadows lengthen, a golden cat crawls out of a crevice between two boulders. She's followed by two spotted cubs. Mom licks them clean and then watches as they chase a grasshopper.

Meet the COUGAR.

A cougar is also called a mountain
lion, puma, panther or catamount.

She's adaptable and will make her home
anywhere there's food and shelter.

She prefers to live alone but sometimes she'll
share a meal with the male in her territory.

She doesn't give up easily, sprinting after her
dinner and even crossing rivers to find food.

She's a great long-distance jumper
and likes to pounce with outstretched
paws onto the back of her prey.

Climbing up trees and
cliffs is no problem.

PREY:

Deer is her favorite food, but she will hunt anything she can catch.

moose

beaver

hare

porcupine

grasshopper

marmot

raccoon

coyote

HOW TO DRAW A COUGAR'S COAT:

Reddish gold fur, black-tipped ears and a long, black-tipped tail. Cubs have spots on their coat which disappear as they grow.

DO COUGARS ROAR?

No, but they do purr.

RANGE:

Mountains, deserts, forests and coastal wetlands of northwest, Central and South America.

Would you like to draw a **cougar**?

No, her coat is too plain.

Overhead, brightly colored birds and monkeys caw and shriek in the trees as we paddle downriver through the rapids. The current slows as we round a bend. On the bank, a beautiful spotted cat noses her two cubs into the shallows for a swim. With a splash, she pounces and hooks a fish with her paw. She drops it on the sand for her cubs to practice eating slippery, wriggly food.

Meet the JAGUAR.

She lives alone with her cubs and will defend them fiercely.

She has night vision but will hunt day or night.

Her jaws are powerful and can crack the hide of a crocodile or the shell of a turtle.

A tree is a great place to stalk prey, eat or take an afternoon nap.

Swimming across rivers is no problem. She loves the water.

She likes to surprise and pounce on her prey, killing it with one bite to the back of the neck.

PREY:
She is not fussy.
Anything she can catch!

peccary

capybara

fish

crocodile

DO JAGUARS ROAR?
Yes, they do, but they can't purr.

 RANGE:
The forests and grasslands of the southern USA and the tropical rainforests and wetlands of Central and South America.

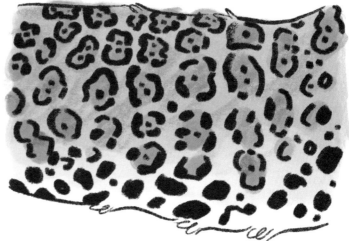

HOW TO DRAW JAGUAR ROSETTES:
Unlike leopards, jaguars usually have small spots within larger rosettes. Jaguars can be black with gray-ish-black markings and are sometimes called panthers.

*Would you like to draw a **jaguar**?*

No, her fur is too soggy. But I think I know who my favorite cat is now.

deer

caiman

monkey

tapir

He has the rosettes and spots of a leopard and the stripes of a tiger.

He loves pouncing...

purring...

and posing for his picture.

But most of all, he loves cuddles.

Meet the other WILD CATS.

There are another 30 wild cat species in the world. Let's meet them too!

AFRICA

🐾 AFRICAN GOLDEN CAT
🐾 CARACAL

🐾 **SERVAL**
Unusually large ears and long legs for leaping on prey. Roams South Africa.

🐾 **SAND CAT**
Lives in the Sahara and Arabian deserts. Catches venomous snakes for dinner.

🐾 BLACK-FOOTED CAT
🐾 AFRICAN WILDCAT

ASIA

🐾 **CLOUDED LEOPARD**
Smaller than the other leopards. Special ankle joints enable him to climb down a tree headfirst and hang off a branch upside down!

🐾 SUNDA CLOUDED LEOPARD
🐾 ASIAN GOLDEN CAT
🐾 BORNEAN BAY CAT
🐾 FISHING CAT
🐾 FLATHEADED CAT
🐾 JUNGLE CAT
🐾 LEOPARD CAT
🐾 MARBLED CAT

🐾 **RUSTY-SPOTTED CAT**
The smallest and most secretive wildcat in the world. Roams forests and grasslands in India and Sri Lanka.

🐾 PALLAS CAT
The longest and thickest fur of any cat. Hunts on snowy mountain plateaus.

🐾 CHINESE MOUNTAIN CAT
🐾 ASIATIC WILDCAT

EUROPE

🐾 EUROPEAN WILDCAT
A small, shy wildcat living in the forests of Scotland and Europe.

NORTH AMERICA

🐾 BOBCAT
A common wide-ranging cat with a stubby 'bobbed' tail.

CENTRAL AND SOUTH AMERICA

🐾 OCELOT
Agile tree climber, ranging from Texas to the Amazon.

🐾 ANDEAN CAT
🐾 GEOFFROY'S CAT

🐾 JAGUARUNDI
Unusual rusty gray-brown coat. Roams forests from Mexico to Argentina.

🐾 KODKOD/GÜIÑA
🐾 MARGAY
🐾 PAMPAS CAT
🐾 NORTHERN TIGER CAT/ONCILLA
🐾 SOUTHERN TIGER CAT

KEY

🐅 TIGER
🦁 LION
🐈 LYNX
🐆 BLACK PANTHER
🐆 SNOW LEOPARD
🐆 CHEETAH
🐆 JAGUAR
🐆 COUGAR

GREENLAND

ALASKA

CANADA

UNITED
STATES
OF
AMERICA

SOUTH
AMERICA

Where are the
EIGHT BIG CATS?

ARCTIC CIRCLE

SIBERIA

RUSSIA

IROPE

CHINA

JAPAN

AFRICA

INDIA

AUSTRALIA

Sizing up the biggest CATS

Measurements of the largest recorded male in order of body weight. Typically, females are 10–30% smaller. Size varies considerably within a species depending on the region.

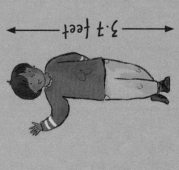

← 3.7 feet →

Average 6-year-old

LYNX

Length of body: 4 feet
Tail length: 0.75 feet
Height at shoulder: 2.5 feet
Weight: 66 lbs

SNOW LEOPARD

Length of body: 4.5 ft
Tail length: 3.2 ft
Height at shoulder: 2.32 ft
Weight: 119 lbs

CHEETAH

Length of body: 4.9 ft
Tail length: 2.6 ft
Height at shoulder: 2.5 ft
Weight: 158 lbs

COUGAR

Length of body: 5.2 ft
Tail length: 2.6 ft
Height at shoulder: 2 ft

BLACK PANTHER

Length of body: 3.5 ft
Tail length: 3.6 ft
Height at shoulder: 1.96 ft
Weight: 198 lbs

JAGUAR

Length of body: 5.57 ft
Tail length: 2.6 ft
Height at shoulder: 2.4 ft
Weight: 264 lbs

LION

Length of body: 8.2 ft
Tail length: 3.5 ft
Height at shoulder: 3.4 ft
Weight: 551 lbs

TIGER

Length of body: 9 ft
Tail length: 3.6 ft
Height at shoulder: 3.6 ft
Weight: 661 lbs

How to stay safe in
BIG CAT TERRITORY

Most big cats are shy and aren't interested in humans unless we put ourselves directly in their path.

When visiting lion, tiger, leopard, cougar and jaguar territory, it's best to go in a group led by a wildlife guide. Snow leopards, cheetahs and lynx are not dangerous to people if we keep a respectful distance.

WHEN ON A JEEP SAFARI

- 🐾 Always stay inside the vehicle. Big cats in Africa and India are used to safari vehicles and ignore them
- 🐾 Don't make loud noises or use flash photography. A big cat might become annoyed. They have sensitive hearing and eyesight
- 🐾 Don't carry or offer food. Cats have a super sense of smell, and you don't want to smell like dinner!

WHEN CAMPING

- 🐾 Always zip up your tent day and night
- 🐾 Don't wander out of camp without a camp security guard, not even to go to the toilet
- 🐾 Don't store food in or near your tent

WHEN HIKING

- 🐾 Be alert to your environment. If you see a big cat, slowly move away
- 🐾 NEVER TURN YOUR BACK and DO NOT RUN. The cat might think you are prey. All big cats can run faster, climb and swim better than people can
- 🐾 If a big cat approaches or charges, they are testing what you will do
- 🐾 Stand still and stand together
- 🐾 Look the cat in the eye
- 🐾 Raise your arms to look bigger and shout, clap, roar and whistle so the cat thinks you're scary and dangerous and not worth the bother
- 🐾 Move away slowly, keeping eye contact with the cat all the time until the cat loses interest

TO LEARN MORE ABOUT BIG CATS

World Wildlife Fund for Nature: https://www.wwf.org.uk

Born Free: https://www.bornfree.org.uk

Big Cat Conservation: https://www.nationalgeographic.org/projects/big-cats/

Big Cats Wild Cat, education, conservation, advocacy: https://bigcatswildcats.com